ANY WHICH WAY

David Watson

The first performance of this production took place at the Only Connect Theatre, 32 Cubitt Street, London, WC1X 0LR on 3 November 2008

A shorter version of *Any Which Way* toured London schools during June 2008

The running time is approximately one hour with no interval

ANY WHICH WAY

David Watson

SYLVIA	Clare Perkins
BAYO	Lanny Wilkie
AKIN	Phillip Clarke
STEFAN	Kareem Dauda
TYRONE	Andrew Brown
SARAH	Alicya Eyo
LEROY	Vinnie Martin
CHORUS	Junior Miller
YOUNG AKIN (on video)	Jacob Talbot
YOUNG STEFAN (on video)	A J Eyoma
GIRL IN PLAYGROUND (on video)	Marnie Rose Duke
Director	Maggie Norris
Co-Director	Emma Kruger
Video Designer	Mic Pool
Designer	Anna Bruder
Lighting Designer	Kristina Hjelm
Composer & Sound Designer	Kath Gotts
Fight Director	Kate Waters
Producer	Joanna Morgan
Production Manager	Richard Seary for Giraffe
Stage Manager	Richard Llewelyn
Make Up Designer	Sarah-Lou Packham
Technical Support	Julian Parmiter
Press Representative	Stephen Pidcock (+ 44 (0) 7984711724)
Press Consultancy	Brunswick Group LLP
Production Photographer	Catherine Ashmore
Promotions	milk two sugars
Graphic Designer	Wayne Summers
Box Office Managers	Jessica Davies, Clare Goring

CAST

Lanny Wilkie now plays the part of Manny, and **Doreene Blackstock**, the part of Bayo.

Doreene Blackstock *Bayo*

Theatre includes: *Noughts and Crosses* (RSC); *The Container* (Edinburgh Fringe Festival); *One Under* (Tricycle Theatre); *25/7* (Talking Birds); *I Have Before Me A Remarkable Document Given To Me By A Young Lady From Rwanda* (Finborough); *The Gift* (Birmingham Rep Studio/Tricycle Theatre); *Downfall & The Carver Chair* (Contact Theatre); *Leave Taking & Girlie Talk* (Belgrade Theatre); *Rosie & Jim's Big Theatre Adventure* (Oxford Playhouse); *Leonora's Dance* (Cockpit Theatre); *Devil Going to Dance* (Birmingham Rep); *Beauty & The Beast* (Tic Toc Theatre Company); *The Children* (Theatre of Black Women); *Top of the Box, The Under 11s Writers' Festival '00, The Westminster Prize '01 & '98* (Soho Theatre).

TELEVISION INCLUDES: *Trinity; Wire in the Blood; Holby City; Judge John Deed; Dalziel & Pascoe; The Dark Room; Casualty; The History of Tom Jones; The Foundling; Common as Muck; Gimme, Gimme, Gimme; The Bill.*

Film includes: *This Year's Love.*

Radio includes: *I Have Before Me A Remarkable Document Given To Me By A Young Lady From Rwanda.*

OTHER PRODUCTION CREDITS

Costume Supervisor Stella Cecil

Polyx-Oil Rapid Matt Washable Floor Sealant sponsored by

osmo

Nick Dudman's non-stain Stage Blood sponsored by Pigs Might Fly

And thanks to Gbolahan Obisesan, Pret A Manger and National Theatre Armoury Department

Only Connect's dishwasher and microwave kindly supplied by

BIOGRAPHIES

ANDREW BROWN – Tyrone

For Only Connect: *Grapes of Wrath*, *Any Which Way* (schools' tour), and *Coming Out from the Cold*.

PHILLIP CLARKE – Akin

For Only Connect: *Any Which Way* (schools' tour) and *Coming Out from the Cold*.

KAREEM DAUDA – Stefan

For Only Connect: *Jitney*, *Grapes of Wrath*, *Any Which Way* (schools' tour) and *Coming Out from the Cold*.

ALICYA EYO – Sarah

Trained: The Court Theatre Training School.

Theatre includes: *Cockroach, Who?* (Royal Court Theatre), *A Midsummer Night's Dream* (Chelsea Arts Centre), *Twelfth Night* (Chelsea Arts Centre) and *Living Under One Roof* (Nottingham Theatre Royal).

Television includes: *Casualty, The Bill, Holby City, Doctors, Hetty Wainthropp Investigates* and *Bad Girls* (five series).

Film includes: *G.M.T, Stalin My Neighbour, Tube Tales and B.U.S.T.E.D.*

VINNIE MARTIN – Leroy

For Only Connect: *Jitney*, *Grapes of Wrath*, *Any Which Way* (schools' tour), and *Coming Out from the Cold*.

JUNIOR MILLER – Chorus

For Only Connect: *Coming Out from the Cold*.

CLARE PERKINS – Sylvia

Trained: Rose Bruford College of Speech and Drama.

Theatre includes: *Generations of the Dead* (Young Vic), *Mules* (Royal Court Theatre), *Ready or Not* (Theatre Royal Stratford East), *Two Women* (Soho Theatre), *Tales from the Terraces* (King's Head Theatre), and *Our Country's Good* (Nuffield Southampton).

Radio includes: *The Lamplighter* (Radio 3), *The Coup* (Radio 4), *Westway* (BBC World Service Drama), *Small Island* (Radio 4), No. 10 (Radio 4).

Television includes: *All In The Game, My Wonderful Life* (three series), *Family Affairs, Men Behaving Badly, The Bill, Holby City, Casualty.*

Film includes: *Bullet Boy* (dir: Saul Dibb), *Secrets and Lies* (dir: Mike Leigh), *Ladybird, Ladybird* (Ken Loach).

LANNY WILKIE – Bayo

For Only Connect: *Coming Out from the Cold.*

DAVID WATSON – Writer

David's play *Flight Path* opened at the Bush Theatre in 2007, in a co-production with Out of Joint, before touring the country and was shortlisted for the John Whiting Award. Other plays include *Just a Bloke* (Royal Court), and *Undercarriage* (Birmingham Rep). He has written short pieces for Paines Plough, Nabakov, and Old Vic New Voices.

Television and radio includes: *L8er* (Hiatus/BBC). David was one of the writers on BBC Radio's Sparks project 2008.

For Only Connect: *Coming Out from the Cold.*

ANNA BRUDER – Designer

Trained: Central Saint Martins College of Art and Design.

For Only Connect: *The Grapes of Wrath* and *Of Mice and Men.*

Other theatre includes: *The Water Diviners Tale* (BBC, The Royal Albert Hall); *The Enchanted Pig, Sleeping Beauty, Skellig,* and *Roots* (Young Vic Theatre Company); *Mannequin* (Barbican Theatre); *Hotel Baltimore, Market Boy* and *Best little Whorehouse in Texas* (ArtsEd).

Assistant Designer to Ian MacNeil: *Vernon God Little* (Young Vic), *Tintin* (Barbican), *Peribanez* (Young Vic) and *Afore Night Come* (Young Vic); to Zaha Hadid: *Pet Shop Boys World Tour,* and to Shunt Theatre Company: *Tropicana* (London Vaults).

Film Art Direction: *Yesterday We Were In America* (Carbon Media Limited).

KATH GOTTS – Composer and Sound Designer

Kath studied Philosophy and Psychology at St Hilda's College, Oxford, and then went on to study music at Goldsmiths' College, London. With

Michael Walton she has written the theme and incidental music for four series of *Bad Girls* on television and the theme music for children's TV drama *The Fugitives*. She has also written songs for characters within episodes of *Bad Girls*, *Family Affairs* and most recently *Waterloo Road*. She composed the incidental music for Peter Flannery's adaptation of *Therese Raquin*, *The Bodies*, at Live Theatre, Newcastle. In August 2005 she and Maggie Norris set up Big Broad Productions Ltd to co-produce *Bad Girls - The Musical*, for which she wrote the music and lyrics. *Bad Girls* was produced at West Yorkshire Playhouse in June 2006 and then in the West End at the Garrick Theatre in Autumn 2008. The show is soon to be released on DVD and a tour is being planned for 2010.

KRISTINA HJELM – Lighting Designer

Trained: Rose Bruford College of Speech and Drama.

Theatre includes: *Edward II* (Eyestring Theatre Company), *Meltdown* (Rambert Dance Company), *MIE* (Cathrine Kontz), *Pagliacci* (English Touring Opera), *Guernica* (Theatre Lab Company, Oval House Theatre), *The Race* (Gecko, international and national tour), *30 000 Lies* (site specific 24 hour performance installation in Turin, Italy), *Venice Preserved* (Arcola Theatre), *She* and *In between ...* (Meghan Flannigan Dance Company, The Place and Laban), *Restricted Area, The Dark Room* and *22 Rooms* (site specific performances by F2, Athens, Greece), *Always* (Mkultra, BAC), *As It Is* (Gary Rowe Dance Company, Arcola Theatre).

EMMA KRUGER – Co-Director and Director of Only Connect

Emma has eleven years' experience teaching Drama and English in London schools and prisons. She has a degree in Drama with English from Manchester University, including work in the TIPP (Theatre in Prisons and Probation) Centre, and a post-graduate certificate of education from the Central School of Speech and Drama. In 2004–05, Emma was the London Director of BBC RaW Stories, the pioneer project in the BBC's literacy campaign RaW (Read and Write). She founded Only Connect in 2005.

For Only Connect: *Jitney* (HMP Wormwood Scrubs), *Steel Magnolias* (HMP Holloway), *Of Mice and Men* (HMP Wormwood Scrubs), *The Grapes of Wrath* (Only Connect), *Coming Out from the Cold* (Only Connect) and with Maggie Norris *Any Which Way* (schools' tour).

MAGGIE NORRIS – Director

Since graduating from London University with a degree in Drama and Dance, Maggie has worked as an actress, a writer, and most recently as a director and producer.

For Only Connect: *Any Which Way* with Emma Kruger (schools' tour).

Recent theatre includes: *Bad Girls – The Musical* at the West Yorkshire Playhouse and its transfer to the West End at The Garrick Theatre. It was through her research into women's lives in prison that Maggie became involved with Only Connect.

Other theatre includes: *The Sunshine Boys* (West Yorkshire Playhouse); *The Bodies*, a new adaptation of *Therese Raquin* by Peter Flannery, with Jill Halfpenny (Live Theatre); *Daisy Pulls it Off* (Duke's Playhouse), *Teechers* (Duke's Playhouse), *Dust* (BAC), *Josephine* (BAC/Oldham Coliseum/UK No 1 Tour – Critics' Circle Award Best Production), *The Father* (Lyric Studio Hammersmith) and *The Assignment* (Old Red Lion).

Film: Executive Producer *Mrs Ratcliffe's Revolution*, starring Catherine Tate and Iain Glen, based on her own experience of being the youngest child of communist parents who, when most people were trying to get out of East Germany, decided to move in.

MIC POOL – Video Designer

Mic is currently Director of Creative Technology at West Yorkshire Playhouse.

Video designs include: *Bad Girls The Musical* (West End/West Yorkshire Playhouse), *Der Ring des Nibelungen* (Royal Opera House, Covent Garden), *The Wooden Frock* (Kneehigh), *The Lion, The Witch and the Wardrobe, The Wizard of Oz, Johnson Over Jordan, Crap Dad, Scuffer, How Many Miles To Basra?* (West Yorkshire Playhouse), *Dangerous Corner* (West Yorkshire Playhouse/West End), *Singin' In The Rain* (West Yorkshire Playhouse/National Theatre/UK tour), *The Turk In Italy* (ENO). *The Ring Cycle* (New National Theatre Tokyo), *Il Tabarro, Chorus!* (WNO), *Of Mice and Men* (Mind the Gap).

Television video design includes: *Lesley Garrett and Friends At The Movies* (BBC).

Mic also works as a sound designer and was the first sound designer to receive a Tony Award for the Broadway production of *The Thirty Nine Steps* (Tricycle/West End/Broadway).

KATE WATERS – Fight Director

Kate is one of only two women on the Equity Register of Fight Directors and works regularly in regional theatre all over the country.

Recent theatre includes: *WarHorse* (National Theatre), *Romeo & Juliet* (Theatre of Memory), *Turandot* (Hampstead), *Forty* (Hackney Empire), *As You Like It* (Watford Palace) *Hamlet* (Shakespeare @ the Tobacco Factory, Bristol) directed by Jonathan Miller.

Other theatre includes: *Don't You Leave Me Here, The Lion, The Witch & The Wardrobe, Macbeth, Safe, Tender Dearly, To Kill A Mockingbird, The Duchess of Malfi & Foxes* (all West Yorkshire Playhouse); *Cracks In My Skin, Who's Afraid of Virginia Woolf, Mary Barton, Separate Tables* and *Kes* (Manchester Royal Exchange), *Little Women* (Duchess, London West End), all the fights for Shakespeare @ The Tobacco Factory (Bristol) including *Macbeth* and *The Changeling* which transferred to The Barbican, *The Lonesome West, Private Lives* and *Mice of Men* (Theatre by the Lake, Keswick), *Oliver, Great Expectations, Kes* (New Vic, Stoke), *Cyrano de Bergerac,* (Nuffield Theatre, Southampton), *A View From The Bridge* (Bolton Octagon), *The Children of the Crown* (Nottingham Playhouse) and *Animal Farm* for the Peter Hall Company.

JOANNA MORGAN – Producer

For Joanna Morgan Productions: *Rabbit* by Nina Raine, Old Red Lion Theatre, transfer to Trafalgar Studios, West End, and Brits off Broadway Festival at 59E59 Theatre, New York. Nina Raine won the Evening Standard Award 2006 for Most Promising Playwright, the Critics' Circle Theatre Award 2006 for Most Promising Playwright and was nominated as Best Newcomer by the Whatsonstage.com Theatregoers Choice Awards. *The Things Good Men Do* by Dan Muirden, Old Red Lion Theatre.

Other theatre includes: *'Tis Pity Shes A Whore* by John Ford, Southwark Playhouse (for which Mariah Gale for her performance as Annabella won the Critics' Circle Theatre Award 2005 for Most Promising Newcomer, the Time Out Award 2005 for Best Newcomer, and the Ian Charleson Award 2005); the worldwide Cheek by Jowl tour of *Othello;* UK big-top tour of *Glastonbury* by Zoe Lewis, designed by Damien Hirst; Declan Donnellan and Nick Ormerod's Academy Company 2002 and its production of *King Lear* for the RSC.

For further information please email info@joannamorganproductions.com.

ONLY CONNECT

'Only Connect!
Only connect the prose and the passion
and both will be exalted . . .'

E M Forster, *Howards End*

Every month 1500 prisoners are released into London. Two-thirds are reconvicted within two years. Half of all crime is committed by ex-offenders.

The reasons for re-offending include the **prose** – practical obstacles to resettlement – and the **passion** – emotional damage and negative attitudes.

Only Connect is a theatre company and resettlement charity working with prisoners, ex-offenders and young people at risk of crime and exclusion.

We connect the **prose** and the **passion**: we use theatre and the arts to transform attitudes, bringing truth and empathy up from the depths, instilling the disciplines of teamwork, taking direction and working towards a goal; and we convert these attitudes into constructive steps towards accommodation, employment and financial stability.

We have staged three productions in prisons with inmates as cast and crew: *Jitney* by August Wilson (HMP Wormwood Scrubs, 2006), *Steel Magnolias* by Robert Harling (HMP Holloway, 2006), and *Of Mice and Men* by John Steinbeck (HMP Wormwood Scrubs, 2007). So far in 2008 we have staged two productions starring ex-offenders at our venue in Cubitt Street, WC1: *The Grapes of Wrath* by John Steinbeck and *Coming Out From The Cold*, a new piece about leaving prison commissioned by Only Connect from David Watson. In summer term 2008 we toured a shorter version of *Any Which Way* by David Watson, commissioned by Only Connect to tackle knife crime, to 17 London secondary schools, reaching 3,600 students.

Alongside our theatre productions we work with our members – prisoners and ex-offenders – to prepare for release and adjust to life outside. We provide ongoing support and advice with housing, benefits, debt, training and work.

Only Connect represents a safe and supportive community for ex-offenders and their families. We host family days and weekly evening meals for our members and supporters, which include structured discussions on spiritual or ethical topics. We offer regular one-to-one sessions, counselling and personal support for our members.

Only Connect fights crime in London by training restored ex-offenders to lead crime reduction projects in local schools and neighbourhoods. We believe that our members have a huge potential for good, with the charisma and personal experience to lead young people off the road that leads to prison. Ex-offenders are the secret weapon in the fight against crime.

In January 2008 Only Connect took possession of the former church at 32 Cubitt Street with generous support from the Goldschmied Charitable Settlement. This is now our base for all our work with prisoners, ex-offenders and young people.

Our thanks to: Tom and Cecilia Amies, Jonathan Benda, Michael and Jane Bretherton, Tracey Campbell, Ben and Zanna Crow, Jessica Davies, Andrew and Angela Deacon, Abigail Deacon, James Duke, Georgia Duke, Marnie Duke, Rebecca Farrow, Eleanor Fellowes, Asa Goldschmied, Dan Goldschmied, Marco and Andrea Goldschmied, Clare Goring, Prue Leith, Jody and Kirstie Wainwright

Telephone 0845 370 7990, *email* info@onlyconnectuk.org
or go to www.onlyconnectuk.org

This production would not have been made possible without the extremely generous support of the following sponsors:

theguardian

John Lewis Partnership

StPancras INTERNATIONAL

Shelagh Anne Venning Trust

The original schools' touring production of *Any Which Way* was made possible by a donation from the Camelot Foundation

Special thanks to:

Father Alexander and St Patrick's Soho Square, Paul Anderson, Victoria Attrill, Toby Baines, Ewen Balfour, Gary Beestone, Antonia Benedek, Rob Brown and Artangel, James Buxton, Tracey Campbell, Bridget Chamberlain, Kath Gotts and Maureen Chadwick, Alistair Green, Phil Hurley, Mark Holmes, Hannah Judge-Brown, Mel Kenyon, Patrick Kerr, Suzy King, Caroline Lewis, Chris McGill, Matthew and Lizzie Morgan, Patrick Murray, Ben Ruse, Anita Scott, Lee Snashfield and Kensal Green Cemetery, Janie Spring. Anna Strongman, Wayne Summers, Sophie Talbot, Alison Wall-Palmer and Canonbury School, Heidi Watson, and

Giraffe
Management for Theatre

Production Credits

Video and Sound Equipment supplied by Stage Sound Services
Lighting Equipment supplied by Sparks Lighting
Washing Machine supplied by John Lewis (Oxford Street)

David Watson

Any Which Way

ff

faber and faber

First published in 2008
by Faber and Faber Limited
3 Queen Square, London WC1N 3AU

Typeset by Country Setting, Kingsdown, Kent CT14 8ES
Printed and bound by CPI Antony Rowe, Chippenham, Wiltshire

A CIP record for this book
is available from the British Library

ISBN 978–0–571–24814–8

2 4 6 8 10 9 7 5 3 1

This play is for all the actors who have worked on it,
who were so generous in sharing
their stories and experiences

Characters

Sylvia

Bayo

Stefan

Akin

Tyrone

Sarah

Leroy

ANY WHICH WAY

This text went to press during rehearsals,
and may differ slightly from the play as performed.

Pre-show: the audience enter a dark space and are confronted by an intimidating soundscape. There is an echoing piece of grime music, as if coming from a building next door. This is accompanied by a piece of Nigerian choral music. There are echoing voices off, which merge into one another:

Voice 1 He's a pussy-hole, 'memba me tell ya. What you know about that boy there. That boy there. He's a eedyat, that's *any* boy. That's *any* boy, when-time I see that boy yeah I'm a' draw for the shank and just *cut* that lickle puss. Watch. Look and see now, you think some lickle pussy-hole lickle nappy-headed breh's gonna boy me off, and come to *my* endz and start chat 'bout he's some top stuff in the game like, are you mad? Bwoy fi dead. Bwoy fi *dead*. (*Etc.*)

Voice 2 How many times I gotta tell you? What time you call this? Huh? I'm asking *you*. I'm asking *you*. Oh your friends, yeah, your friends, you go out with your friends, you call them friends? You call them friends? You think these people are the people you should be mixing with? Don't shout at me. Don't shout at me. What can I do? What can I do to make you stop? What can I do to make you stop? Tell me. (*Etc.*)

There is video projection of mobile phone footage – the London streets from a teenager's point of view. This cuts to: Stefan and Akin, both aged nine, in one of their bedrooms. One is filming the other, as part of a school homework.

Young Akin Is it recording?

Young Stefan Just shut up and say your ting you know.

Young Akin (*laughing, embarassed*) Oh gosh.

Young Stefan What you waiting for?

Young Akin Stefan how can I do this if you don't even know if it's recording you know?

Young Stefan Just do it man. *Bonjour.*

Young Akin Why you speaking French for?

Young Stefan *Comment . . . Comment tu t'appelles?*

Young Akin What?

Young Stefan What's your name?

Young Akin My name is Akin.

Young Stefan How old are you?

Young Akin I'm nine man. I'm nearly ten.

Young Stefan Yeah?

Young Akin Hold the thing still.

Young Stefan Why?

Young Akin You get shit marks or something like that, give it to me.

Young Stefan Get off man.

Cut to: later. They have calmed down a bit.

Young Stefan What you wanna be when you older?

Young Akin Er. Footballer.

Young Stefan What d'you like to do at the weekend?

Young Akin Er. Swimming. Watching TV. Like . . . playing football. Er. Nah, like when I'm older I'm either gonna be a footballer or a dentist like but. It's more . . . better to be a footballer though innit.

Young Stefan Why?

Young Akin I dunno.

The footage freezes, and Sylvia speaks.

Sylvia 'Pon the twenty-seventh October 1988, him pop out a' me belly and me whole life change. Rain a' fall. And him bawl and him wail but him beautiful. And true him a' we first born, and every parent love them first born wid a special kind a' love, some pure kind a' love. And him grandfarda say, 'If the pickney come out a bwoy he musse name after him farda.' And him cousin say, 'Nah, we call him Michael, after my man Jackson innit.' But me say, 'No.' Me say, 'Stefan.' Me hold him inna me arms and me say, 'Stefan. Only Stefan ago do it.'

Bayo speaks.

Bayo They say that God made the country and man made the town. But London is a place made by God nor man. When you step off the plane, you see a greyness as far as the eye can see. I turn around. I look at my son. 'Akin, are you OK?' He is four years old. When he is a big man, he will take the greyness for granted. Do I want this? Is this the way? It takes courage. To hold him by the hand. To step off the plane, and put him into this grey world.

Sylvia From him farda die Stefan grow cold. Him vex me sometime. And when him born the doctors them call him premature, 'ca true seh him born out a' me three weeks early, but as him grow him always late – 'Is why them call you premature when always you a' reach late?'

Stefan Mum.

Sylvia 'Mum?' How you mean, 'Mum'?

Stefan Mum, 'low it, I'm here now yeah?

Sylvia Backside, wha'ppen to the children nowadays?

Bayo The children nowadays. Akin was different once, but now he is the same. Now we are in London he has the greyness inside of him. I tell him this, he does that. All I want is the best for him, and all he does is the worst.

Akin Dad, I told you before, I don't like you being in my face.

Bayo Come here and speak to me.

Akin I'm gone yeah?

Bayo Where are you going?

Sylvia Where you a' go? Me want fi know wha'ppen to my son. Some time we share the same blood, same bone. Now me can't see what you want from the world.

Footage of Stefan and Akin in the street, surrounded by onlookers –

Stefan I want you to look me in the face now and tell me what you're going on with like, what you a' tek this ting for?

Akin Blud, Stefan, move from out my face yeah 'ca your breath come smelly y'nuh, you just stink out the whole place like.

There is laughter and jeers from the onlookers.

Stefan Are you tryin a' boy me off? Are you tryin a' boy me off? Do you know about me? How long you know me for? How long you know me for man?

Akin Blud, ten pound ten bag, wha'ppen to you, you come beggin favours now.

Stefan Man ain't beggin from no man.

Akin What, come check me some next day y'nuh me nuh inna this foolishness.

Stefan Oi don't walk away from me. Don't walk away from me.

Akin You're a pussy-hole. You're a pussy-hole.

They start to fight. There are shouts from onlookers. Stefan stabs Akin.

Tyrone's place. Stefan bursts in on Tyrone. Tyrone is clutching a letter.

Tyrone Yes fam. See it deh?

Stefan Help me.

Tyrone You know what this is blud?

Stefan Hush your mouth and come here.

Tyrone Poppi' champagne!

Stefan Shut up.

Tyrone Nah man. The last time me feel this good y'nuh me win the Duke of Edinburgh Award.

Stefan Tyrone.

Tyrone looks at him and sees he is covered in blood.

Tyrone Oh nah nah nah. What you done?

Stefan Come here.

Tyrone What you done man, this is deep. Oh gosh.

Stefan Shut your mouth before I bang you over.

Tyrone Wha'ppen to you man? You look mash up.

Stefan I stabbed some boy.

Tyrone What boy?

Stefan You need to know my business now?

Tyrone Stefan I swear your business is my business you know.

Stefan You think 'cos you're my cousin I won't stab you up the same way?

Tyrone Bruv.

Stefan Gimme some clothes before I bang you out. Move.

Tyrone (*getting clothes*) I just wait on a day like today sometimes.

Stefan Yeah well the day just come. Are you happy now?

Tyrone No.

Stefan You think I'm having that? Some pussy-hole lickle nappy-headed breh tryin a' boy me off?

Tyrone You kill him?

Stefan What you ask me some foolish question for?

Tyrone Swear down. You should know what you done.

Stefan I don't know!

Beat.

Tyrone Gimme them things, I throw them away.

Stefan What, are you dumb? You need to take them and burn them, you don't put 'em in no rubbish bin.

Tyrone Well take them off my floor man. My mum cleaning up from morning.

Stefan Dickhead.

Tyrone Where you gonna go?

Stefan I dunno.

Tyrone Will you text me?

Stefan (*laughs*) Shut up. Pass me my phone.

Tyrone does so. Stefan smashes the phone.

Tyrone What you do that for?

Stefan I don't want feds on my tail man. I'm on the D-low from now on.

Tyrone I can't believe you done this you know.

Stefan Yeah well take a look down the road 'ca there's a ute down there just painting the pavement all red. See what you believe then.

Tyrone Shit man.

Stefan Where's your money?

Tyrone Man ain't got no money bruv.

Stefan I ain't gonna ask you again.

Tyrone I'm telling you man.

Stefan grabs him.

Please. Please. I beg you please man. Stefan.

A police siren passes nearby. Stefan lets him go. Beat. Stefan grabs a bag of weed.

That's my weed you know.

Stefan Did I tell you not to smoke this?

Stefan starts skinning up. Tyrone picks up the letter.

Tyrone You see Monday yeah? I got a job interview you know.

Stefan Is it.

Tyrone Yeah, football coach, 'a me that, what you know about that? And I wanted you to . . . come help me with. . . what to say and all them tings there, now . . . everything messed up.

Stefan Stop crying.

Tyrone I'm not crying.

Beat.

Stefan You're some lanky boy you know. Your clothes too big for me.

Tyrone Buy your own then innit.

Stefan I gotta go see Sarah.

Tyrone What you gonna tell her?

Stefan What you think I'm gonna tell her?

Beat.

I wake up this morning I see clear you know that? I don't feel no . . . boring pain just deep in my stomach, I feel free. I feel live. 'Ca I'm bigger than anything. Today's a big day for me.

Tyrone Stefan.

Beat.

What d'you feel?

Stefan How you mean, what I feel?

Tyrone I don't like the way you're going on like. You should feel bad for what you done.

Stefan laughs. Beat.

Stefan You know what yeah, don't even bother follow after me. When I think about you I feel ashamed you know that? Eedyat.

Footage of Stefan making his way to Sarah's place. Distorted echoes of the childhood scene in the background.

Sarah's place. Stefan and Sarah.

Sarah He's dead.

Stefan Who is?

Sarah You think you can just duck out and no one'll know it was you?

Stefan I ain't ducking out.

Sarah What?

Stefan I said I ain't ducking out, I got places to go. True you ain't from round here you know, you dunno how it goes.

Sarah Oh yeah, tell me how it goes then.

Stefan (*laughs*) You think some boy's gonna snitch on me? You mad?

Sarah If the police don't come for you someone else will.

Stefan Yeah bring them. Come man I'm ready.

Sarah What d'you come round here for?

Stefan What d'you mean?

Sarah What I say.

Beat.

Stefan You're my girl innit.

Sarah Is it? Don't feel like it. We don't talk about things, you don't call me. When you go out you're out on road. With your 'boys'. Come knocking on my door three in the morning 'cos you can't get the business somewhere else.

Stefan What you talking about?

Sarah What was his name?

Stefan Who?

Sarah The boy you killed. The boy you put a knife into and bled dry. Or don't you know?

Stefan What's it matter, ting's done now.

Sarah Ting ain't done, nothing ain't done.

Stefan You don't know him.

Sarah Tell me.

Stefan Akin.

Beat.

It was Akin.

Beat.

What?

He moves to her.

Oi what, you need to help me.

Sarah Take your hand from me, don't touch me.

Beat.

What, you see him die yeah? You watched him?

Stefan Oh I wish you could understand the place I'm coming from. See how you might be tight with someone from day yeah, but sometimes people switch. Like, you think I'm having someone boy me off like that, I don't care how long I know them from. People need to understand what I'm gwarnin' with, like. If you was there, then you would know like, I'm bigger than him, I'm bigger than anything –

Sarah Just shut up.

Stefan I see clear now you get me I see clear. (*Laughs.*) I come from Tyrone just now, he's a pussy-hole, he's the biggest dick on road. And in this world yeah, you either turn pussy-hole, or bad man.

Sarah Oh yeah, which are you?

Stefan Come with me.

Sarah (*laughs*) 'Come with me.' Where you gonna go?

Beat.

Stefan When you think about your life yeah what's it make you feel?

Sarah What you asking me that for? What d'you care?

Beat.

Stefan You ever know your dad?

Sarah Course I know my dad.

Beat.

Stefan What, you ever feel you need to reach him you know where to find him yeah?

Sarah Yeah, my dad's house.

Stefan Yeah well, my dad's house six feet under the ground now, y'understand me? Getting all cosy in the soil, where all the worms at.

Sarah So?

Stefan So it's kind a' hard for me to reach him down there you know but I feel like I need to go and chat to him or something like that. Yeah me and him will talk.

Sarah Are you buzzing?

Stefan Shut up.

Sarah Don't tell me shut up you little dick. Yeah, Daddy's dead, and what? You just sent him some boy to keep him company.

Stefan slaps her hard across the face. A beat.

Stefan Look what you made me do. You see what happens when people get me mad? Whole world just turn their back on me from day like, I get boyed off by school, I get boyed off by my bredrins –

Sarah Can't you see that it's you? Always going on about . . . it's school, or it's people, or it's olders or it's youngers but it's you! You're the only one whose steppin' in your shoes.

Beat.

Stefan Where's your money at?

Beat.

Sarah, gimme some money before I bang you over.

He grabs her, she struggles.

Sarah Stefan!

He manages to grab her purse, and takes all the money out of it.

Stefan Everyone turn their back from day but I don't care. I'm bigger than anything.

Sarah What's the matter with you?

Stefan I'm gone yeah.

Sarah Yeah, you're gone yeah, go. Don't come back. I hope the police come and shoot you in your head.

Footage of Stefan making his way from the flat. Voices over the top of this.

Voice 1 When we was their age, we knew how to be rowdy. Back a' the bus, ghetto blaster. They got music on their phones now. They got music everywhere they go.

Voice 2 See the drugs started coming in the seventies and the guns in the eighties. Now we're all playing against a different backdrop.

Voice 3 If a kid did something naughty he stood out. Now a kid'd have to do something more than naughty. Have to do something notorious. Kid'd have to put his soul on the line.

Voice 1 Mrs Wilton?

Voice 2 Mr Ojemji?

Bayo Yes?

Sylvia Wha' you want?

Voice 1 Please sit down.

Bayo May I ask what the problem is, Officer?

Sylvia Wha' you want from me?

Voice 1 It's about your son.

Voice 2 It's about your son.

Bayo I know, that he has been –

Voice 1 There's been a stabbing.

Sylvia Him dead?

Voice 2 I'm so sorry.

Voice 1 Do you know where Stefan is, Mrs Wilton?

Sylvia Is why you look at me that way for? Like is me who stabbed the bwoy. Like is me who put the knife inna him hand and seh, 'Galong deh go kill that ute deh.' Wherever Stefan do, him can do off him own mind, you hear me? That bwoy feel-say him can do anyting him want.'Ca me put him out.

Bayo Officer there will be no rest for the man who has taken my son. If I will live in pain then he must feel the same pain. (*Beat.*) Oh gosh. (*Beat.*) I would like to find the man and see why he has done this. (*Beat.*) I do not know why the world has come . . . so cold. And I do not know why Akin is the one to die, and I am the one to live.

A scrap of wasteland. Leroy enters. He is drinking from a bottle and eating fried chicken.

Stefan enters.

Leroy Mawga bwoy!

Stefan (*not looking at him*) What's happening?

Leroy Backside, you come like duppy.

Stefan I'm just passin' tru man, wha'ppen to you?

Leroy You a' 'pass tru'? Come sit down over ya-so.

Stefan I told you already.

Leroy Come nuh man. You like fried chicken? Where them fry it up inna the fryer, and the man them seh, 'That a' the fried chicken fi go run tings y'nuh,' and the woman them seh, 'Blouse and skirt, a' my favourite chicken that –'

Stefan Bruv, you look like you pulled out a bin.

Leroy From your belly full then you can cuss me. But from you're hungry . . .

A beat. Stefan comes and sits next to him.

Yes my ute.

Stefan You stink.

Leroy (*offering his hand*) Leroy.

Stefan Yeah? (*Beat.*) Stefan.

Leroy Yes, Stefan. Top-a-top chicken nyammer. Him nyam up the chicken from the finest dustbin inna the area.

Stefan spits the chicken out.

A' joke me a' mek wid you boss.

Stefan Shit man.

Leroy Time fi cool out y'nuh. The weather nice. Everyting alright.

Stefan Is it.

Leroy Wha'ppen to your hand?

Stefan I fell over innit.

Leroy 'I fell over innit.' You fight somebody?

Stefan No.

Leroy Somebody fight you?

Stefan Maybe you should watch your own business you know.

Leroy Bwoy, Stefan, cool nuh man. A' chat me a' chat wid you y'nuh, me nuh inna the gully-gully ting deh.

Stefan Yeah, watch your mouth and watch your stinky breath too yeah?

Leroy Cha. (*Beat.*) Me can see you is a man where you just know where you want, eeh?

Stefan Believe.

Leroy I going drink to you.

He offers the bottle to Stefan, who shakes his head. Leroy kisses his teeth, and drinks. A beat.

You nuh come from round here?

Stefan No.

Leroy Is which part you come from?

Stefan North. I come from far innit. I walk all the way here. I spend my money on clothes so I have to walk.

Leroy Wha' your T-shirt name?

Stefan That's Evisu innit.

Leroy Seen.

Stefan What, you like that? That's moneys bruv.

Leroy Why you a' come over ya-so?

Stefan I told you already man, I'm passin' tru.

Leroy Well, nuff people a' pass tru, but true seh more time them a' know seh where them going to next, seen?

A beat.

Stefan You know where Kensal Green Cemetery is?

Leroy Kensal Green?

Stefan Yeah.

Leroy Cemetery?

Stefan Yeah.

Leroy No. (*Beat.*) But from you gimme five pound . . .

Stefan I told you man I ain't got any money. I got the shirt on my back.

Leroy Is it. (*Beat.*) Is what you running from?

A pause.

Stefan Yesterday. In the afternoon. (*Beat.*) I got bare mad you know. I stabbed some boy.

Leroy Him dead?

Stefan I dunno. Yeah. (*Beat.*) When he laid out on the road he come like a baby like. Just limp.

Leroy Is wha' him to do you? That you stab him so bad?

A beat.

Stefan When I ask the man for weed yeah he blanks me. Like we ain't grown up together or something like that. Like we ain't known each other from . . . four years old. People shouldn't boy me off like that.

Leroy So you stab a one bwoy, and now you want go to the cemetery and stab him again?

Stefan What you talking about?

A pause.

When I think about stuff I feel angry you know. (*Beat.*) My mum . . . always fighting me down from day like, Come we just do what we wanna do innit. I don't wanna do this, do that, read Bible now, go church now, clean my room now, later man.

Leroy Wha'ppen to your farda?

Stefan He's dead.

Stefan sighs. He puts his head in his hands.

Leroy Come nuh bwoy. Come. Stefan. (*Beat.*) Me can see-seh you is a bwoy where you can go any which way, seen? (*Beat.*) You come so *far*. You *walk*. (*Beat.*) And true seh you done suttum, where you don't know which way fi turn. (*Beat.*) Life never come natural fi we, y'understand? Life come strange sometime.

Stefan dries his eyes.

Stefan I feel bad you know.

Leroy watches him. A beat.

Leroy You feel shame.

Stefan Yeah.

A beat.

Leroy You feel angry.

Stefan Yeah.

A beat.

Leroy Frightened. (*Beat.*) You know why?

Unnoticed, Leroy has pulled out a huge knife.

Because you a' pussy-hole.

Stefan Shit.

Stefan tries to run but Leroy grabs him. There is a struggle, which ends with Leroy holding the knife to Stefan's throat.

What you doing man?

Leroy Shut your bumba-hole bwoy.

Stefan Please.

Leroy From you say another word I going cut your throat seen?

Stefan Please man I ain't done nothing to you.

Leroy 'Please man'? You come inna fi-we area and start chat 'bout you a' big man, when you're just a lickle *puss*!

Leroy smacks Stefan's face into the ground.

Stan' up. Stan' up rude bwoy.

Leroy kicks him. Stefan slowly stands up as Leroy laughs.

Tek off your T-shirt.

Stefan Nah man.

Leroy Y'have money for me? Tek off your T-shirt.

Stefan takes off his T-shirt. Leroy grabs it and punches him.

'Mummy!' Tek off your jeans and say, 'Mummy! Why you don't love me Mummy? Why you don't care for me?!'

Stefan spits out some blood.

Me can't hear you!

Stefan Mummy.

Leroy Wha' you a' seh?

Stefan Why you don't love me Mummy?

Leroy Jeans!

Stefan slowly takes his jeans off.

Stefan Why you don't care for me?

Leroy grabs the jeans.

Leroy Yes my ute. Stan' up. Look at me. (*Beat*) Look at me, seh, 'My name is Stefan, and I am a pussy-hole.'

A beat.

Me can't hear you. (*Beat.*) Speak nuh man. (*Beat.*) Speak!

Leroy punches him in the face.

Stefan My name is Stefan.

Leroy Wha' you a' say?

Stefan My name is Stefan, I'm a pussy-hole.

Leroy Huh?

Stefan I'm a pussy, I'm a pussy-hole!

Leroy laughs.

Leroy Galong deh. G'weh.

Stefan starts to crawl away.

Your mudda and your farda should recognise you now. You come naked as the day you did born.

Leroy drinks. He laughs.

'Help me Mummy!' 'Please Mummy!' 'Why you leave me 'pon me own?'

We hear an African spiritual.

Over this, footage of the young Akin, trying to recite a poem he has written.

Young Akin
I like to lie in my bed to sleep,
But if I can't sleep, then maybe I will eat.
But there is not nothing to eat . . .

I like to lie in my bed to sleep,
But if I can't sleep then maybe I'll eat,
But if I can't sl— eat . . .
Oh shit.

Bayo Death is cruel, and so is life. Life goes on. Life forgets. People say words to me, and I say words to them. I think of words I must say to you. But then I remember that you are gone, and I will never say words to you again.

Photos of Akin in the mortuary.

What will they do to you now? They will break your bones and put you in a box. And we are the ones, who must carry our own broken bones.

Sylvia's house. Sylvia and Sarah. A pause.

Sylvia Well me lay up two places deh 'pon the table still. (*Beat.*) 'Ca true seh he might just . . . turn up and . . . bang and slam the door behind him. And just sit down and eat up my food inna my kitchen. (*Beat.*) Like nuttin nah gwam.

Beat.

Sarah Maybe he'll do that.

Beat.

Sylvia When him farda die. Lord. A' three years we still a' set the table fe him. And we know seh him dead and bury. (*Beat.*) And we know seh him will never reach again. (*Beat.*) Not even for him breakfast, much less dinner.

Beat.

Sarah Did you feel . . . ?

Sylvia Mmm?

Beat.

Sarah Did you feel sad?

Beat.

How long did you feel sad for?

Beat.

Sylvia Tek your finger from out a' your mout' child, a' pickney me 'a talk to?

Beat.

When's your birt'day?

Sarah Monday.

Sylvia Is how old you ago turn?

Sarah Twenty.

Sylvia Twenty. Lord. (*Beat.*) When I did turn twenty we go over to the dance over Portland. 'Ca Portland bwoy deh just sweet us them time there. (*Beat.*) But them nuh like fi see the St Mary people over Portland 'ca them say St Mary people come wid all the fussing and the fighting and is really that we come like bad breed. (*Beat.*) Like the air over St Mary come different. Like we just poisoned by it.

Sarah He never meant to kill him.

Beat.

Sylvia Him tell you so?

Sarah No. (*Beat.*) But I know that it's true though.

Beat.

Sylvia And . . . And when . . . And when you a' finish this one course you a' deal with, you . . . Are you going to apply for . . . another course?

Sarah I don't know.

Beat.

Sylvia Well. (*Beat.*) Think-say you haffi make up your mind soon eeh? Or . . . (*Beat.*) Time ago run. (*Beat.*) Time ago run and catch you.

Sarah I don't like the course. (*Beat.*) I don't find it interesting. (*Beat.*) I find it boring.

Beat.

Sylvia Wha'ppen to my son? (*Beat.*) You can tell me? (*Beat.*) 'Ca the teachers them duss him out from nineteen-how-long, and them still nuh tell me. And the policeman 'all a kick down the door from five 'a clock a' morning and and and tek him go police station and bring him back and them still nuh tell me. (*Beat.*) And Stefan. Stefan don't seh nothing to me. Him bawl and him holler and cuss me. But him don't seh nothing. (*Beat.*) Him silent.

Sarah Stefan thought that you was . . . strict on him. Too much. Sometimes. Like, that he couldn't do what he wanted.

Sylvia And so him tek up a knife and go stab him best frien'? And kill him dead?

Sarah He gets mad sometimes.

Sylvia If him can't hear him ago feel. A' so me a' raise Stefan. A' so me mudda raise up me, and her mudda raise up her.

Sarah Do you love him?

Sylvia Why you ask me some foolish question child?

Beat.

Sarah I thought that . . . sometimes he couldn't tell. Or something like that.

Beat.

Sylvia Stefan musse wanted a next mudda to me. (*Beat.*) 'Ca him never smile. Never show me kindness.

Sarah I think that he would like to. (*Beat.*) I think he'd like to a lot.

Beat.

Sylvia From him reach again. Or . . . me just a' tek the clock inna me hand and turn back the time deh 'pon it so . . . tings nuh come like them come. (*Beat.*) I would beg. And beg. And beg Stefan. (*Beat.*) Fi just turn weh. Fi just turn round 'pon the road where him walking.

Beat.

Sarah Maybe it's not too late.

Beat.

Sylvia A' no one life Stefan dash weh when him put the knife to that young bwoy deh. Lord. (*Beat.*) Him just tek my life inna him hand and him kill me dead.

A graveyard. Stefan sits by his father's grave. The ghost of Akin enters and watches him. A beat.

Akin Oi blud. Blud. Who that pussy-boy deh?

Stefan Oh shit. Please man. Please.

Akin No it ain't 'please'. It's 'sorry'.

Beat.

Stefan Akin.

Akin That's my name, don't rinse it.

Stefan You scared me y'nuh.

Akin Yeah I know this.

Stefan What you doing creeping round a graveyard?

Akin What you doing creeping round a graveyard?

Beat.

Stefan You look rough.

Akin I'm dead innit.

Stefan Oh yeah.

Akin Some weak-heart put a shank in me.

Stefan I'm not a weak-heart.

Akin Yeah? If you're not a weak-heart you're a pussy.

Stefan Don't call me pussy, man.

Akin I can call you what I want, you know. Come like you're my bitch now, you know that? 'Ca you owe me for this.

Stefan Don't owe you for nothing man, move.

Akin Oh, you don't owe me nothing, OK.

Beat.

Stefan Are you a ghost?

Akin I dunno you know. Must be. Man gets stabbed over some little thing like, that's deep.

Stefan You shouldn't boy me off like that. You're my bredrin.

Akin Why you come along beggin' some discount price nonsense, a' wha that?

Stefan Why you selling weed for anyway?

Akin Blud, I'm not the one going on like super-thug. So from I get on just some lickle hustle ting now you get jealous?

Stefan You think you're rolling with bad man? Them man there wasteman.

Akin Stefan you might be on some one-man soldier ting but I roll *deep*. You get me, I roll with my family.

Stefan They ain't your family.

Akin We move tight.

Stefan You move tight yeah? Well come see how many a' them crying tears for you, now you're gone. Yeah I'll show you how tight you was.

Akin Shut up.

Beat. Stefan indicates the gravestone.

Stefan You know who that is?

Akin No.

Stefan S'my dad innit.

Akin Rah! Is he dead?

Stefan Nah man, he's just having a lie down. Course he's dead.

Akin Shit man. I forget he died you know.

Stefan Yeah. (*Beat.*) First time I come here innit. When he died I never come. 'Cos I didn't feel to or something like that. Didn't come to the funeral or nothing like.

Akin My funeral's gonna be live, mate.

Stefan Yeah?

Akin People all singing, dancing. My funeral's gonna piss on all the other ones you know. Swear down.

Beat.

Yeah, I feel sorry for my dad though. 'Ca when I was alive, I was just angry with him innit. Now . . . (*Beat.*) I feel bad.

Beat.

Stefan People thought my dad was African innit.

Akin (*smiles*) Yeah, yeah.

Stefan 'Ca he used to wear all the . . . robes and all that. (*Beat.*) Yeah, he was big in the community like. Going round the old people. Checking up on them. (*Beat.*) Never really spent . . . too much time with us though. Like we wasn't good enough. (*Beat.*) Like he was disappointed.

Beat.

Akin There's so much things yeah where I wanna do but I can't do them now, y'understand?

Stefan Yeah well, get over it. (*Beat.*) What's it like? Being dead.

Akin It's long. More prefer to . . . be alive innit.

Beat.

Stefan I think about you all the time.

Akin Chi-chi man.

Stefan Serious. Sometimes I just think . . . why did I do that? I feel stupid.

Beat.

Akin Oi. Look and see now.

He rolls up his T-shirt to reveal his stab wound.

Yeah?

Stefan Does it hurt?

Akin Touch it. (*Beat.*) Go on.

Stefan touches the wound – Akin shouts in pain.

Stefan Shit!

Akin (*laughing*) No, jokes, jokes, jokes.

Stefan You're a dickhead, man.

Beat.

Akin You see you yeah, you're the kind a' guy where you can go any which way. Y'understand? And you're the only one who can decide that.

Stefan Too late now.

Akin What?

Stefan I said it's too late now innit.

Akin Nah 'low that talk. Ain't never too late. Too late for me innit. I'm just pushing up daisies out here. But you? You got your whole life in front of you, you know. I feel jealous.

Stefan Maybe. (*Beat.*) Are you mad at me?

Beat.

Akin Boy. Sometimes.

Stefan If I was you I'd be mad.

Akin laughs, softly.

What?

Akin You need to buy some clothes, you little tramp.

Stefan You need a wash man.

Akin Shut up. (*Beat.*) Everything that I can't do you need to go forward and do that for me innit.

Stefan Whatever, man.

Akin Standard. (*Beat.*) Now move yourself before feds come.

Stefan I feel scared, you know.

Akin Yeah you should be. (*Beat.*) Oi Stefan.

Stefan What?

Akin Don't forget about me.

Beat.

Stefan No I won't, man.

Replayed footage of previous events – the childhood scenes, the murder, the journey etc.

During this Tyrone enters, and paces, in an abandoned church. He looks like he is muttering to himself.

The footage stops, and Tyrone talks to an invisible enemy.

Tyrone A' me you a' talk to?

Eh?

Is who you a' talk to?

A' me you a' talk to?

Well, me can't –

Well me can't see anybody else deh 'bout 'ya y'nuh, A' me you a' talk to? Yeah? Yeah?

He pulls out a chocolate bar and holds it like a gun.

Pussy-clart, wha' you ago do now you lickle fassy? Bad man time, yeah? Yeah?

Sarah has entered, unnoticed.

Sarah Yeah bad man time!

Tyrone Oh shit.

Tyrone quickly starts eating the chocolate bar, as casually as he can.

Sarah What's happening, Tyrone?

Tyrone Alright? Yeah, nothing, just . . . chilling out and them ting there.

Sarah Right.

Tyrone Yeah yeah. You see the police chopper?

Sarah Yeah man.

Tyrone It's mad innit.

Sarah Yeah.

Tyrone Just proper . . . flying around.

Sarah What you doing in here?

Tyrone Boy. Me and Stefan used to come in here innit. When we was young.

Sarah Is it.

Tyrone Yeah, used to be a church, but. Boy. Now it's all mine.

Sarah It's nice.

Beat.

Tyrone You feel better today?

Sarah Little bit.

Beat.

Tyrone Yeah, you look better.

Sarah Yeah?

Beat.

Tyrone Yeah, you look good.

The doors are flung open and Stefan enters. A beat.

Yes fam.

Stefan (*subdued*) How you doing, Tyrone?

Sarah So it's true then.

Stefan What is?

Sarah 'Stefan reach.' Big knife man, back inna the area.

Tyrone They got a chopper out for you, y'nuh

Stefan Yeah, I see it.

Sarah Where did you go?

Stefan Away. (*Beat.*) London's big you know. Bare heads.

Sarah Why d'you come back?

Beat.

Tyrone She asked you a question.

Stefan Tyrone, go chicken shop, buy me some chicken yeah?

Tyrone Blud.

Stefan I'm hungry.

Tyrone The last time I do this you know.

Stefan Believe.

Tyrone exits. A beat.

I went to find my dad's grave innit.

Sarah That's nice.

Beat.

Stefan All pigeon-shitted out. Grass all growing over it. Looked like any grave man.

Beat.

Sarah Your mum gone in all the papers. Saying for you to turn yourself in.

Stefan Yeah, she washed her hands with me from day.

Sarah Yeah, and you done the same to her.

Stefan True she'd love to see me in my little cell, my one bed, my one chair. Yeah, I feel-say that's exactly where she wants me.

Sarah She thinks you done bad. Now you pay.

Stefan Yeah, and what d'you think?

Beat.

Sarah I think . . . (*Beat.*) I think d'you care about anyone? (*Beat.*) 'Cos I'm twenty today you know that? (*Beat.*) And when he laid out in the road. They said he looked like he was sleeping.

Stefan moves towards her. He holds her. A beat.

Stefan I feel empty sometimes.

Sarah I don't know who you are.

Stefan You know me, man. (*Beat.*) You know me.

A beat. He kisses her. Tyrone re-enters. He groans as he sees them kissing.

(*To Tyrone.*) Bring me some food.

Tyrone Police deh 'bout y'nuh.

Stefan They're following me.

Sarah They know you're here?

Stefan Not yet.

Tyrone How you mean, 'not yet'?

Stefan eats, quickly.

Stefan I'm gonna have to go away for a bit. And you're gonna be on your own for a while. But you can deal with that innit.

Tyrone Stefan, it ain't me you should be worried about.

Stefan What you mean?

Sarah I need to talk to you.

Tyrone She carrying news for you!

Sarah Tyrone!

Stefan What's he talking about?

Tyrone Tell him.

Beat.

Sarah Gonna be Mr Responsibility now, yeah? (*Beat.*) Yeah, I'm gonna have a kid.

Beat.

Stefan What, mine?

Sarah Yes, yours.

Beat.

Stefan You sure?

Tyrone Course she's sure, she pissed on the ting and everything.

Beat.

Stefan You just make my life complicated you know that?

Sarah Oh yeah, you make my life simple? My babyfather's gonna be a jailbird.

Tyrone Yeah and what, my dad banged up from I was two years old, ain't nuttin wrong with me.

Stefan Shut up.

The sound of the police helicopter is getting closer.

Beat. Stefan holds Sarah. He feels her stomach.

You scared?

Sarah No. Are you?

Stefan Mate, I'm always scared.

A police siren wails in the distance.

Tyrone The pair a' yous need to go y'nuh, just take a couple things and take some money and splurt.

Sarah What you gonna do?

Stefan Stay away from me yeah, I just bring badness on people.

Tyrone Stefan.

Stefan Did you get your job?

Tyrone I dunno.

Beat.

Stefan What, football coach yeah?

Tyrone Suttin like that.

Stefan When you gonna know?

Tyrone I dunno blud, I don't even want that anyway like, I'm not on some bow-cat six-pound-an-hour rubbishness.

Stefan Do that, man. Just get a job and just do your thing. Work your way through. Everything that I can't do you need to go forward and do that for me innit.

Beat.

Sarah Stefan, you need to move.

Stefan Will you wait for me?

Beat.

Sarah Wait for you what?

Stefan Will you wait for me though?

Tyrone Stefan.

Beat.

Stefan I wake up this morning I see clear, you know that? (*Beat.*) Today's a big day for me.

The helicopter and sirens rise to a crescendo, and we hear police voices echoing from a loud-hailer. Other voices echo out:

1 He was on his way to the West End to buy a cable for his Xbox.

2 He came to Edmonton from the Congo at the age of thirteen, but his life became dominated by gang violence and robberies.

3 He came from Afghanistan to escape the conflict.

4 The last time I saw him he said that he'd found God, and that he wasn't on no hype ting any more.

5 He was a happy boy, with a bubbly personality, who never let his circumstances get in the way of anything.

6 He was part of Kilburn's SD crew, which stands for 'Street Dreamz, Street Disciples, Street Dealers'.

7 He wanted to be a lawyer.

8 He was a gentle giant, who his father said had 'an innate decency'.

9 He was an aspiring young actor, who had already appeared in the latest *Harry Potter* film.

10 She was a popular, friendly and well-behaved girl who had much to contribute to our school community.

11 He said that he didn't want to die, and called out for his mother.

12 He was the kind of boy teachers looked forward to having in their class.

13 He came from Ghana six years ago and hoped to become an engineer.

14 He had a passion for bikes and motorbikes.

15 He was two years older than me, but he still used to look out for me at playtime, or in the summer holidays.

16 He had been watching a film at the Showcase Cinema in Beckton.

17 He was stabbed five times, while others attacked him with baseball bats.

18 Everything is different now he is gone, and Streatham is no longer live without him.

19 She was vulnerable and sweet and harmless and I'm not just saying this.

20 She was stabbed in the heart after trying to stop an argument.

21 He was a member of the 'Penge Block' gang, and used the street name 'Swipe'.

22 Everyone remembers his cheeky little smile.

23 He was stabbed in the leg when he moved to protect his friend.

24 He refused to hand over his phone, and was stabbed in the stomach.

25 He was caught up in a fight between two rival gangs in Stoke Newington.

26 Two months after he died, his GCSE results were released. He gained two Cs, three Bs and one A.

Sylvia Stefan!

Bayo Akin! Akin!

Sylvia Stefan, don't make me shout again!

Akin Stefan, come we play football yeah?!

Tyrone Stefan! Wha'ppen to you?!

Bayo Akin!

Sylvia Stefan!

Stefan I'm coming man.

Tyrone Stefan!

Bayo Akin!

Beat.

Akin.

Reprised footage of Young Akin and Young Stefan.

Young Stefan What you wanna be when you older?

Young Akin Er. Footballer.

Young Stefan What d'you like to do at the weekend?

Young Akin Er. Swimming. Watching TV. Like . . . playing football. Er. Nah, like when I'm older I'm either gonna be a footballer or a dentist like but. It's more . . . better to be a footballer though innit.

Young Stefan Why?

Young Akin I dunno.

The End.